NETWORK MARKETING

How to Gat Started and Successed in Network Marketing

(The Most Complete Blueprint for Success)

Roger Watson

Published By Roger Watson

Roger Watson

All Rights Reserved

Network Marketing: How to Gat Started and Successed in Network Marketing (The Most Complete Blueprint for Success)

ISBN 978-1-77485-391-7

All rights reserved. No part of this guide may be reproduced in any form without permission in writing from the publisher except in the case of brief quotations embodied in critical articles or reviews.

Legal & Disclaimer

The information contained in this book is not designed to replace or take the place of any form of medicine or professional medical advice. The information in this book has been provided for educational and entertainment purposes only.

The information contained in this book has been compiled from sources deemed reliable, and it is accurate to the best of the Author's knowledge; however, the Author cannot guarantee its accuracy and validity and cannot be held liable for any errors or omissions. Changes are periodically made to this book. You must consult your doctor or get professional medical advice before using any of the suggested remedies, techniques, or information in this book.

Upon using the information contained in this book, you agree to hold harmless the Author from and against any damages, costs, and expenses, including any legal fees potentially resulting from the application of any of the information provided by this guide. This disclaimer applies to any damages or injury caused by the use and application, whether directly or indirectly, of any advice or information presented, whether for breach of contract, tort, negligence, personal injury, criminal intent, or under any other cause of action.

You agree to accept all risks of using the information presented inside this book. You need to consult a professional medical practitioner in order to ensure you are both able and healthy enough to participate in this program.

TABLE OF CONTENTS

INTRODUCTION 1

CHAPTER 1: WHAT EXACTLY IS NETWORK MARKETING? ... 4

CHAPTER 2: WHAT TO UTILIZE YOUTUBE TO REACH A LARGER VIEWERSHIP AND ESTABLISH TRUST WITH VIEWERS 11

CHAPTER 3: MINDSET 19

CHAPTER 4: THE BEST WAY TO RESEARCH A BUSINESS OPPORTUNITY 31

CHAPTER 5: AND THE STORY CONTINUES 56

CHAPTER 6: THE MISTAKES TO AVOID 76

CHAPTER 7: STRATEGIES TO GROWING YOUR BUSINESS. 96

CHAPTER 8: DISCIPLINED THOUGHTS 118

CHAPTER 9: PROMOTION OF THE EVENTS 143

CHAPTER 10: NETWORK MARKETING TIPS, STRATEGIES AND TRICKS THAT WORK 150

CHAPTER 11: KEEP FOCUS ON COMPETITIVE LANDSCAPE 159

CONCLUSION 178

Introduction

This book is aimed at aiding you to start your own successful business of network marketing by ensuring that you make sure you're wildly successful. By following the advice and tips that are provided in this book, you can quickly advance in your business and eventually be a top earner. This book was created to help those who are committed to creating huge success in their businesses and with their teams. If this is you then you're at the right spot.

Contrary to other books that advocate tactics that are sloppy and flimsy the book will train you to become a natural business leader. Since, my dear you're managing a real company and it is right to be run in a professional manner. You won't be taught about the unproductive and sometimes embarrassing methods which are being promoted in the network marketing community that is not educated. Instead, you will to become an enthralling leader who draws leads with ease.

In each chapter, you will be taught about a specific aspect within your enterprise that's essential in achieving your goals. Learn how to create an effective foundation using branding strategies that will give you the best chance to begin your business of network marketing that will be successful.

In the next step, you'll discover effective lead-generation strategies that can literally draw customers to you. As opposed to having to chase them down to convince clients to become part of your company or purchase your product and services, they will be beg to join! This is among the most rewarding aspects of being a business leader. You avoid being restricted in the "employee" mentality and are able to assume the "leadership" position that will have a major impact on your company. This book will show you precisely how to accomplish this.

Furthermore, you'll be able discover how to sell your items and grow your business. In essence, you're going to be taught the essentials you must be aware of in order to achieve success in your business. This book will show you how to begin with the basics and continue to increase your business's earnings success. If you're ready to be a leader and achieve massive success in your business of network marketing and are eager to study Network Marketing: The Complete Guide on How to Build an enduring Network Marketing Business Using Online strategies and techniques (Learn proven online and social Media techniques that will propel your business to the next level).

Chapter 1: What Exactly Is Network Marketing?

Network marketing, also known as multi-level marketingis an popular business model that allows ordinary individuals to create their own business. It operates by using one distributor working in conjunction with a variety of people who are referred to as independent distributors. Independent distributors are sales representatives of the company and are accountable for their own performance in the industry. Each of them pay for an "start-up package" that includes all the equipment they require to begin selling for the distributor. They use their expertise to market the product to clients, and then recruit distributors, referred to as"down-line" "down-line".

This business model is loved due to its versatility and the potential. In many network marketing businesses independent distributors aren't required to buy any inventory or stock, therefore they do not have to produce any funds prior to earning money out of their initial costs. Also, the principal distributor or the company itself is the one who holds the stock, and the distributor sells it and the company fills the orders. Due to this, the majority of distributors are online, or use catalogues that are distributed at events.

Distributors have a variety of levels of potential within their network marketing businesses. They could remain distributors, selling to their family and friends to earn a small income, or create a whole team and create an empire. Through their empires they could create an enormous income stream that, if constructed correctly requires very little effort to manage and maintain. There are various levels that distributors are able to achieve that are determined by the size of the team and sales worth. In many cases, to be eligible for an "promotion" or move higher, a distributor has to be in a certain number of distributors within their downline, and also a certain amount of income per month. It is a good thing that if you employ the strategies you'll learn from this book to establish a steady team and the customer base that will make this simple to accomplish.

Contrary to what many believe it isn't an ad-hoc scheme. While there are many levels, it doesn't work in the same manner that an actual pyramid scheme and it's actually a legitimate and accepted business model. In contrast to a pyramid scheme network marketing is an actual company and funds are paid to purchase goods. When pyramid scheme schemes are used, the money is given in installments to"ring leaders "ring chief" and false assurances are made that every person in the pyramid will receive a specific amount of money. In the network market, funds are transferred to the business at the top. In contrast, the independent distributors are basically

Network marketing has grown into an extremely popular business opportunity for all ages. Parents who stay at home and working people, those with work constraints ambitious entrepreneurs, retired people and many more are getting into network marketing as it's a fantastic method to boost your earnings and generate streams of income that are passive. Anyone could benefit from this lucrative business opportunity since it's an effective way to boost your earnings while also contributing to your financial security.

You may be thinking why some companies prefer the model of a network marketing company instead of typical brick and mortar storefronts. It's simple, as independent distributors have an opportunity to have an affordable start-up and so do major distributors. Instead of having to pay the huge costs of building construction and expenses, such as the cost of their employees and other expenses, they can develop a brand or product line, and then shift into network marketing. In this way, they could manufacture their goods, manage an order fulfillment and shipment center, then let the independent distributors handle the job for them. Instead of paying hourly wage for their "employees" they pay commissions on what their independent distributors generate in sales. They also receive a lot of free marketing as their independent distributors market their own strategies to grow their teams and sales. This is a great cost-effective opportunity for everyone that is involved.

Network marketing was first introduced at the mid-1800s. This was when J.R. Watkins was founded. In the mid-1800s, J.R. Medical Company decided to establish a natural remedies company and utilized network marketing as a way of selling their products. In the years since, the scope that network marketing is grown and hundreds of major distributors have popped up on the market, with their own independent distributors. Network marketing isn't an entirely new method. It's actually an established and tried-and-true method of business that has been proven to be successful for many repeatedly. The book's intention is to ensure it is successful for you too!

For individuals to be successful in the field of networking marketing, people must an understanding of the business processes. It is essential to understand how to market products, lead the team, and manage the other fundamental business tasks in order to keep things running smoothly. It will take some effort initially however, once you've got the hang of it, you'll be able to effectively manage a business from your home through your network marketing company . it could earn you income in the comfort of your bed!

Chapter 2: What To Utilize Youtube To Reach A Larger Viewership And Establish Trust With Viewers

Since YouTube is a medium for visuals It is highly recommended to use YouTube to the maximum extent in the development and implementation of your digital marketing strategy.

Advertising in YouTube's marketplace, like 30-second or 15-second commercials can be a great way to increase your profile online and targeting particular audiences in the digital age. The cost for buying an YouTube advertisement spot is calculated per-view. Advertisers pay per view of every advertisement, which could range between $0.10 and $0.30. A further benefit of using the YouTube advertising system is every view of your advertisement counts towards your entire YouTube views. In turn, you can also increase the number of views on the YouTube channel by purchasing an advertising space and reach an enormous public. Similar to other social media platforms, YouTube allows you to focus on a particular age group as well as genders, locations and. In general, marketers must spend more money, on a progressive basis, to target certain niches of people with the use of digital strategies for marketing.

The YouTube's global audience continues to expand. With more and more companies are creating content that is accessible to users through videos, YouTube is a coveted platform for advertisers and marketers who are looking to reach their intended viewers in the digital space. Furthermore, millennials are the most popular demographic to use YouTube. If you're planning on reaching a younger audience with your products or services, YouTube is a great way to ensure that this young target audience is targeted. Additionally, when you use YouTube your reputation and credibility with the public will increase as you'll be seen as an edgy Social Media platform. In turn, this increases your trust with viewers, improving your ability to turn viewers to loyal customers of your company and generate more income.

The most effective way to begin using YouTube to reach a wider audience is to set up your own YouTube webpage for your company. The page is extremely beneficial in allowing you to make the content you want to create without the need to outsource marketing expenses to a third party company or increase your budget to an enormous amount. Additionally, this page allows you to choose telling your story using an extremely well-known visual medium that connects with younger viewers specifically. Rememberthat the purpose of creating content is creating content that differentiates it from competitors. With YouTube and, specifically the YouTube page for your company it is possible to reach your viewers on a regular basis by using a relevant medium.

For a reasonable cost, YouTube advertising is an ideal way to improve your online presence and gain an even larger audience for your company. For companies, especially, viewers actively engage with your promotional content as it isn't an uninteresting advertisement. It can be extremely enjoyable if you can incorporate the imagination in your material. Indeed, this broadening of the number of views received from your audience can help boost the credibility of your company. Additionally, it could increase the visibility of your company while also creating relationships with your intended viewers. Additionally that the additional views on YouTube will increase your impression on the internet. In other words that, with increasing viewings on YouTube from your intended viewers as well as the new audiences which your content for marketing is attracting, your brand will show up in a higher quantity of organic search results both on YouTube and other search engines which are used by almost all active online users (Google particularly).

When you create content to promote your company on YouTube There is no need to produce an "viral" content. Instead, you'll be in creating content that appeals to your audience with a unique, engaging and instructive manner that highlights the strengths of your business and conveys the impression that your company's offerings are intriguing. This is also true about the way your content demonstrates the particular products or services of your company.

Establishing a YouTube channel to promote your business or brand is a very effective way to increase your reach while communicating your customers the "story" that you tell about your company. This method of marketing offers the chance to constantly educate your clients and customers on subjects that pertain to the company you run. Remember that consistency is key and the most effective content is consistently written, especially when it is related to your company and the products or services it provides.

An excellent tip for making marketing content for YouTube (or or any other platform on the internet in general) is to stay clear from making content that's controversial. This applies to content that is too political or that openly endorse a specific political candidate, social issues that are polarizing and so on. If certain topics divide the population, there's an excellent likelihood that your clients and customers are divided by those issues too. So, make sure you remain dedicated to creating content that is relevant and inclusive to your company's needs and its products or services and the story of your brand.

In the age of digital it is imperative for you to produce content that lets viewers be satisfied. In the present, viewers have become accustomed to instant gratification throughout all aspects in their daily lives. This is particularly when it comes to the media they consume and engage with regularly. This is why the use of visual content on YouTube videos is extremely advantageous for businesses as this method of delivering content and marketing lets you respond to your customers' requirements and benefit of the latest trends in consumer behavior in the current market.

Chapter 3: Mindset

Like any other business setting your goals for success is the most effective way to achieve the success you want in your business. If you think about the differences between successful network marketers and failed network marketers, you will notice generally some obvious distinctions. The ones who are flourishing tend to be positive, enthusiastic and enthusiastic about what they're doing. However people who aren't flourishing are typically less enthusiastic about their product and are more pushy and more anxious regarding their sales. We will discuss how to enter into that mindset for success and the wrong mindset you should avoid to keep from losing potential customers as well as team members!

Embrace Criticism

There are literally hundreds , if not thousands of people who believe that network marketing is a scam and that you'll never succeed in it. However, there are hundreds, if not thousands of people who are thriving and performing phenomenal in their businesses. If you believe that marketing is a fraud are those who will be giving you critiques, calling you names because you are an employee of the business and expressing others who are not happy with your work. Success stories are those who learn to ignore the negative criticism and accept the criticism and go on in spite of it. If you allow the negative and criticism get to your mind, you'll be unsuccessful because you'll be stop before you've even thought the end of it.

Rejection Happens

Rejection is an element of every sales enterprise. If you are employed by the company with an outlet, or you are employed by an telemarketing firm or work for an organization that is a network marketing firm You will encounter rejection. It is essential to realize that rejection can happen and it shouldn't stop you from pursuing your business. Be positive and you'll be able to identify your audience that is interested in your product. The more optimistic and positive you appear, your more customers will flock to you and your product. Do not try to convince those who aren't. Instead, focus on cooperating with the ones who are and aiding them in getting set up with all the things they require.

Be Patient & Persevere

In the beginning, you may not be able to make a significant amount of sales , and your team may not be growing as fast as you'd like. While some appear to be able to increase their business's size immediately but this isn't the situation for every single one of us. The best method to ensure constant growth in your business is to work hard at your company. Don't rush, be patient, and trust your process and work until you see the results you're looking for!

Be Aware of Team-Based Thinking

The key to success with network marketing lies in having an effective team. Your downline and upline are equally important to your particular section of the company. Your upline is the ones who will coach your to succeed, which is why it's crucial to choose those that reflect the sort of success you want to attain in your personal business. Also, your downline is crucial since they are part of the system which helps you to grow as well, the greater you can help them grow and advance your level, the better you will be. As such, it is crucial to be aware of the mentality of your upline and become a good leader for your downline. A team-oriented mindset can help you develop since people will be inclined to collaborate together, as well as your group will be more likely to achieve success. Always focus on networking with your team as well as potential new team members.

Trust the quality of your Company, Your Products, and yourself

It is essential to be convinced in all you do. If you aren't convinced of your product or company then you'll be unable to stand in their stead and even promoting them to other people. Also, if you aren't confident in yourself, you're not going to be convinced that you can build an effective business, and, in turn, you will not. It is crucial that you select a firm that you trust, and you are confident in the products you're using as well. You don't have to be a fan of every product however, make sure that you are a fan of the majority and give each of them a fair chance. So, you'll be able to promote your product because you'll be a fan of them too.

Concentrate on your success

There's a reason so many people believe that manifesting your dreams has such an impact on your chances of success. In reality, focusing on your goals is the most efficient way to reach it. There's an old adage that says "if the car you're driving toward the tree and you concentrate upon the tree you're certain to strike it. But, if you're moving and you concentrate on where you'd like to go, there's a chance that you'll be able to make it happen also." Instead of focussing on the things you don't desire, concentrate on what you really want. Do not fret about the negative comments of others and their fear that you'll fail. Don't let fear of failing demotivate you. Instead, let your vision of what success could appear to succeed. It's a good idea to take time every day prior to starting work in your business to concentrate on what you would like to accomplish. Set your sights on what you wish to accomplish that day and what you would like to accomplish in the near future. In this way, you'll always know the goal you want to achieve and strive to achieve it. It's more effective to focus on things when you know the direction you're headed towards rather than working in a blinded manner away from something you do not wish to. The truth is that the more you pay attention to something, the more likely you are to be able to get it, regardless of whether you'd like it or don't.

Seek out Opportunities

One of the best ways to make sure you're achieving within your business is to seek out opportunities. This is true at all levels: search for opportunities to increase sales and look for opportunities to increase your team's size and look for opportunities to help your team train to handle part of the team's work load, and much more. Each time an opportunity that could lead you to your goal comes along be sure to take advantage of the opportunity. The more you are aware of opportunities to take advantage of them, the more opportunities you will have. While you will have many opportunities to achieve your goals, you will also be more successful because you're constantly striving toward this. Be sure to be seeking opportunities to improve your business, yourself and your personal freedom, so that you don't pass up a opportunity to transform your business into the business you desires. If you're hoping to earn a passive income, develop you business up to the size you want by looking for opportunities. You can make use of every opportunity to help your team members learn how to lead their teams, while you provide support to your immediate team and take advantage of the freedom and benefits of your passive income stream.

Spend Your Time judiciously

It is crucial in establishing an attitude of achievement. There are many ways to invest the time you have in an effective way which will help the growth of your business. In the first place, you must be sure that whenever you do something that is commercial, it will yield enormous outcomes for you. Don't waste time on minor tasks that are not important to your business or your business's success. When you're doing business ensure that you are focused on getting things done and do your best to accomplish as much as you can. A passive income is one which you don't have to spend lots on managing. If you're seeking to transform your marketing venture into passive revenue it is likely that you will be looking to ensure that you don't spend all of your hours attempting to make it happen. Although you'll definitely have to put in more effort in the beginning, you will become more relaxed as you begin to invest your time well into things that bring your dream to life and you'll be able to run a successful business beneath your control! Be sure that all your time working is devoted to either your business's growth, your personal expansion, or your team' development. Make sure you are focused on your business the entire period you work to ensure that there aren't any distractions and you finish quickly.

Recognize Your Success

The most significant aspect of a healthy mental attitude is the ability to be a master of gratitude and positive energy.

One of the best ways to accomplish this is to recognize your accomplishments. Every time you earn sales, increase your team, hold an enjoyable training session or learn something new or perform any other activity that has a positive impact on your success, make sure you take the time to be proud of yourself and your accomplishments! It is also possible to take photos of your joyous occasions and share your photos online to show others how exciting your company is as well as how joyful it makes you. This can cause others to be more interested in creating the same kind of excitement and joy within their own lives! In the end, it's an win-win. Be sure to make time to be proud of the achievements you've made in your company to ensure that it is enjoyable and interesting for you. If you're more satisfied with what you're doing and accomplishing, the more quickly will be able to get into a state of mental clarity that allows you to easily contribute to your company and its development. Soon, you'll be impossible to stop with your business. And within a short time you'll be a top-earning entrepreneur who is able to spend virtually zero time working on the business , yet still earns an amazing source of income from it. That's right, you'll be able to earn a steady stream of income that's making a lot of money for you even while you sleeping.

Chapter 4: The Best Way To Research A Business Opportunity

What is a real business opportunity? The question has been posed by numerous people who are trying to decide whether or not to purchase a currently franchise, an independent company or, as we'll call in this piece as an opportunity for business. To help ease the confusion, we provide an analogy that is simple. Remember elementary school , when your teacher explained the distinction between a rectangle and the square. The square is also an equilateral triangle, however the term "rectangle" doesn't mean it's an exact square. Similar relationships exist between the business opportunity, independent businesses available for sale, and franchises. Franchises and independent businesses available for sale are business opportunities, however none of them meet the requirements of being a franchise , nor do they qualify as in the strictest sense of the term independent businesses available for sale.

What makes matters even more confusing can be the fact that states in 26 have passed law that define business opportunities and regulations for their sales. Most often, these statutes are written with such precision that they incorporate franchises, too.

There are many states that have an opportunity law defines the term the same way. But, the majority employ the following criteria to define the term:

1. A business opportunity entails the leasing or sale of any item, service or equipment. which will allow the buyer-licensee to establish a company.

2. The seller or licensor in a commercial opportunity states that they will help the

buyer to locate an appropriate location or offer products to buyer-licensee.

3. The seller guarantees a revenue that is greater that or equivalent to the amount the purchaser of the license is paying for the product when it's resold . It also guarantees that there exists a market demand in the service or product.

4. The initial amount due to the seller to begin the business opportunity should be between $400-$1,000.

5. The seller of the licensor promises to purchase back any item purchased by the licensee buyer in the event that the product cannot be offered to prospective customers of the company.

6. The products and services created by the seller-licensor can be purchased by the purchaser of the licensee.

7. The licensor-seller for the business opportunity will offer an marketing or sales program to the purchaser of the license, which frequently includes the use of trademarks or trade names.

The law governing business opportunity ventures typically do not permit the selling of an independent company through its owner. They are primarily designed to protect the multi-sales of distributorships and companies that don't comply with the requirements for franchise according to the Federal Trade Commission (FTC) rule adopted in 1979. This law provides business offerings in three forms that include packaged franchises along with product franchises and business opportunities.

To be considered a business opportunity according to the FTC rule, four components must be in place:

1. The person who purchases an opportunity to start a business, usually called a franchisee or licensee, must sell or distribute goods or services offered by the franchisor or licensee.

2. The franchisor or licensor must assist in securing an outlet for retail or accounts for the products and services the licensee is disseminating or selling.

3. There must be a money transaction between the two parties that is at least $500 prior to , or within six months from the date that the franchisee or licensee begins the business.

4. The conditions and terms of the contract between the licensor as well as the licensee should be set out in writing.

It is clear that the selling of opportunities for business as described in FTC rules FTC rule is very distinct from selling an independently-owned company. If you're dealing with sales of independently-owned business the buyer is not bound by commitments to either seller. When the transaction is completed, the buyer is able to sign up to any business operation system that they prefer. There is no ongoing relationship between the seller and buyer. Ventures that offer business opportunities, similar to franchises, are companies that require the seller to make an agreement to maintain a relationship with the purchaser.

The types of business opportunities

The FTC defines the most popular kinds of business opportunities in the following manner:

* Distributorship. It is an independent agent who has entered into an agreement to market and sell the product of a different company but does not have the right to use the company's trade name in

their trade names. According to the terms of the agreement the distributor might be limited to selling the company's products, or have the right to promote various types of products or services offered by different companies.

* Rack jobber. It is the process of selling other companies' products via racks distributed across a range of shops which are managed through the rack jobsetter. Typically the buyer or agent is able to sign an arrangement with their parent business to advertise their products to various stores through strategically placed racks in stores. The parent company acquires various places where the racks are put up on the basis of consignment. It is the responsibility of the agent to keep track of the inventory, shift the products around in order to draw customers, and also to manage the bookkeeping. The agent provides the manager of the store with an

inventory control sheet that outlines the amount of merchandise sold. After that, the distributor gets paid by the store or the location with the rack that is less the commission of the store.

* Vending machines route. Similar as rack jobsbing. The cost of investment is typically higher in this kind of business opportunity because the owner of the business must purchase the machines and the items being offered however, the process is reversed with regard to the payment procedure. The operator of the vending machine has to pay the proprietor of the store an amount based on the sales. The most important aspect of every route arrangement is getting sites in areas that are popular with pedestrians and, obviously that they are as close as is possible. If your destinations are across the globe, you will are wasting time and money managing these locations.

Alongside the three categories of business opportunities that are listed above There are four additional kinds of opportunities you need to keep in mind:

* Dealer. Similar to a distributor , however unlike a distributor who may sell to several dealers Dealers typically sell to retailers or the consumer.

* Trademark/product licenses. In this kind of agreement, the licensee gets permission to utilize the vendor's trade name and specific equipment, methods technologies, or products. The use of the trade mark is completely voluntary.

* Network marketing. It is a broad term that encompasses the entire field of multilevel marketing and direct sales. As an agent in network marketing you sell products via your own network of neighbors, friends or coworkers, and so on. In certain instances you can earn

additional commissions when you recruit other agents.

* Cooperatives. This is like a licensee arrangement where a business like an establishment like a hardware store or hotel may join with an even larger group of businesses similar to it, usually to serve the sole purpose of advertising and promotion with a shared identity.

How Can the Government Protect You

The FTC Rule in force since 1979. been in place since late 1979 and has had a wide-ranging impact on the business and franchise opportunity sector, and potential licensees or franchisees. The rule was designed to assure prospective buyersof an opportunity for business or a franchise that they'll be provided with a full informational document that contains the information necessary in order to take an educated decision about investing.

Despite the FTC's regulations and the active action at the state level, there are a few sellers who are seeking every avenue to get around the rules. It is true that neither the FTC regulation nor state laws cannot guarantee that there is no fraud. This is why you must pay close attention on your FTC disclosure statement given to you.

Anyone who is interested in an opportunity for business must be provided with an FTC disclosure statement at least 10 days prior to signing a binding contract or paying cash (or any other payment) in exchange for a payment to the seller. The requirement of 10 business days is not too much. If you have a face-to-face meeting with the licensor, or a representative to discuss a possible purchase or sale from the opportunity and if the meeting leads to a shrewd selling presentation for the company, then the owner should give you an information document at the moment.

If you're not receiving an FTC disclosure statement Don't sign anything nor give any money away regardless of claims made that it's "refundable."

If the seller fails to provide you a disclosure statement it is in violation of federal law, and could also violate the state law. If the seller claims that his or her product is exempt from FTC rules, ask an opinion letter from counsel prior to engaging with them further. Also , ask the salesperson to provide the number of the state agency in their area or FTC office that has informed them that their offering is exempt. There are very few business opportunity offers that are exempt. The only exceptions are when the total amount paid in the initial six-month period is not more than 500 dollars, or when it is only made to pay for the initial inventory sold at the wholesale price of the product.

Franchises are different from. Business Opportunities

As a general rule an individual franchisee has greater support and assistance from its parent business, is able the trademarked name and is more tightly controlled from the franchisor. Business opportunities are, however aren't given as much assistance from the parent business, typically, they don't have the benefit of a trademarked name and aren't subject to the operating guidelines of the parent company.

As we've mentioned previously that there are a variety of business opportunities. There are some that are turnkey operations like a number of franchises that are packaged. These opportunities offer everything you'll require to begin a business. They will help you choose an area, they provide instruction, they provide support to the licensee's marketing as well as an entire inventory for starting up.

In contrast to a franchise that is packaged, they are business ventures aren't trademarked by companies that are owned by the same parent. The logo, name, and name of the business and the manner in which it's run is the sole responsibility of the franchisee. Often, the sole obligatory requirement for the buyer and seller is that the inventory must be only purchased via the parent corporation. Of course, all of these conditions are listed on the form of the disclosure document and the contract.

The advantages of a business Opportunity

There is a lower fee for the initial investment than franchises. While the number of franchises with low investment has increased, the price to be able to participate in the business world is substantially less. The FTC has a minimum investment to be considered a business possibility, however, there are plenty that meet this requirement but the average is $2,000 to $3,000.

* A well-tested process or product. The systems in place today help to maximize effectiveness and return on investment and reduce difficulties. It's just an issue of passing on knowledge which is still the most effective teacher. If they're honest or not, the majority of people enjoy having their hands sometimes. When things go wrong the parent company is in the position to assist the licensee through the bumps. Many like the idea of security by numbers.

* Training intensive programs. In every new venture there is a significant amount

of time and cash are spent during the initial learning phase. An effective business opportunity will eliminate the majority of unproductive moves with an extensive training program.

* Financing options that are better. Because of its financial strength as well as credit line and contract agreements the parent company that is offering the business opportunity will often offer better financing than a person might be able to obtain. Leverage is an important factor in any investment.

* Professional advertising and promotions. The majority of small-scale business owners do not invest enough money in marketing. If they make an effort, they are usually poorly thought out and inconsistency. Many business opportunities provide buyers with printed advertising advertisements, slicks for radio or TV storyboards. for the purpose of

helping give a more effective marketing campaign. Some business opportunity companies even be able to sign a cooperative agreement in which they share the costs of print advertisements, radio or television. This kind of assistance in marketing is especially useful in large cities where the expense of advertising is too high for the proprietor of a single store.

* Continuous counseling. The majority of business opportunities offer assistance not just via training, but also the assistance of a team of experts that provide help that no individual could ever afford. Legal advice is provided to a certain extent. The most efficient accounting systems -perfect for the particular industry-have been developed by experts in the area. Certain licensors provide free analysis of the records using computers and by comparing them to other systems can

reveal areas of loss or inefficiency as well as profit-making areas of business that aren't being considered.

Assistance with selecting a site. Experts in the field of site selection and marketing select locations using the most advanced technological tools available. Professional negotiators negotiate contracts and leases to the most advantageous advantage, using the influence of a large company to influence landlords and other significant figures.

* Purchasing power. Sometimes the parent company's massive purchasing power and special buying strategies can provide products, equipment , and even products to licensees for less cost than an independent licensee could receive.

* No ongoing royalties. In a business opportunity unlike franchises there aren't

any regular royalties due to the seller. Profits are yours to keep.

The disadvantages of a business Opportunity

If the conditions are right there are business opportunities that can be an excellent, low-risk way to start a the business market with minimal risk and a great chance of success. There is no way to guarantee that everything is perfect, and here are some challenges to be prepared for:

* Poor site selection. Most business opportunities are retail establishments that depend on the location's location, its visibility , and easy access to the business. The majority of people who are interested in business opportunities simply take the places they choose for them. DON'T! Go through it carefully. You could even engage an outside marketing expert to

review and perhaps argue with the parent company's choices. The location you choose could translate into millions of dollars in profit over 20 years.

Lack of continuous support. There's usually no need for the business opportunity vendor to provide ongoing assistance of any type. If the seller chooses not to provide information or guidance to help you once you've established your business then you might not have any recourse to you.

* Exclusion clauses. Are you limited in selling just the merchandise of the manufacturer? If so, and you break the law in any way there is a chance of the licensor rescinding the contract. If you buy from different sources, it can be difficult to hide. The majority of parents will demand that you open up your accounts to examine them at specified intervals of time. Any irregularities will be identified

during these periods. The most savvy purchasers of opportunities for business will agree to the clause in the contract that specifies the source of the supply the event that there is a problem with the product's quality.

* Parent-company bankruptcy. Another danger is the risk that the parent company will overextend its own resources and eventually becoming insolvent. Although this isn't as critical in a business endeavor like it is in the case of a franchise, you are at risk of losing your business due to the fact that your property agreements could have been financed by your parent business.

You must carefully research any business venture you're interested in. Take a list of the company that is parent and contact them. Consult a lawyer about any agreement that is drafted from the company that is parent. You should get a disclosure statement. Be sure to carefully review the licensee. Do not let anyone pressure you. Be sure that a responsible business supports your business idea.

Guideline to help you choose a business opportunity

Be sure that your business opportunity you're considering is in compliance with all the business opportunity laws - which differ from state to state and is registered in the states that require. Find out whether the business opportunity that you're looking at offers buyers with an offer prospectus. If it's a business venture that is covered by the FTC regulation, then the company is mandatory to provide specific information to the buyer.

If you're considering a business venture be aware that if you purchase opportunities from a firm that has a large number of outlets and has been operating for at minimum three years, you'll spend more money for this established model than an opportunity that's newer. If you're thinking of a new business venture You should look into the history of the parent company to determine its performance and longevity in its specific area of operation.

If you asked an expert in business what they would recommend to assess which is "right" commercial opportunity that is right for your needs, you'd likely get these suggestions:

1. Do a fair assessment of your capabilities and self-worth.

If you've worked behind an office for a long time do you feel content reaching out to businessmen and offering them a tangible service? If you've worked as a field salesperson for many years and you're happy selling snacks at an counter?

2. Your business must be run with enthusiasm.

Would you be content to present the world to a brand new product or unique service that the general public has no idea about? Do you have the ability to generate excitement about something that is not widely advertised?

3. You must be knowledgeable about the product or service in which you are involved.

When the company that is parent to you offers the buyer little or no instruction in management or technical knowledge Be wary of the business chance. If the seller of the license has organized all of the operational knowledge into a standard operating guideline be sure to take advantage of the business possibility.

4. Do a market assessment of the service or product to be provided.

Is it time for introducing it to the general public? Does there exist a need for this kind of item and what's its value with regard to the competition?

5. Learn how many customers have been operating with success for a significant amount of time.

An authentic business opportunity can offer you contact numbers for other customers, so that you can confirm that they are generally satisfied with the business opportunity as well as that the vendor is able to fulfill the promises made to them.

Chapter 5: And The Story Continues...

My name is model from 1958 and was raised as the sole kid of parents who divorced. For the majority of my life, I resided with my grandmother who took care of me in a tender and strict manner, and based on her own beliefs. She would always say "Jannie go to school, complete your assignments and pursue a degree and an ongoing job, at least in the banking sector. This way, you don't have to contemplate the possibility of losing your job." It was not my experience to be encouraged to think about the possibility of being self-employed and start my own business. It was not our intention, we were part of the middle class, and that was not any way in the cards. In reality I was never asked what I would like to pursue or what my dream was and what they were if any of those dreams could be fulfilled. I was taught to be a decent and decent girl who followed according to what was taught and who stayed away from excessive attention.

Numbers were never one of my strengths and, therefore, for the obvious reason the idea of a banking degree was not mentioned. However, I was close to becoming an RN because I was born with the desire to help others and, if I could even save the entire world. But , fate intervened and I was married and becoming a mother of two at when I was

Over the years, I've been through a myriad of experiences including being an assistant in the nursery as well as a factory worker, an healthcare assistant as well as a sales assistant an assistant to sales and a sales manager. Also, despite every expectation, I've attempted to be self-employed. My last position for an employer was with Philip Morris, where I was Duty Free

Manager and had oversight of the sales in the duty-free market across Denmark as well as Norway. It was a highly-publicized job that included many trips, "fine wine & dine" as well as a great fixed salary, pension car for the company, as well as many fringe benefits. Naturally, I enjoyed everything however the job did not satisfy my need to be creative. I didn't thrive in the confines of a strict framework that placed the emphasis on administration, lengthy written reports, documents even for the smallest detail that required a lot of decision making and a high-stakes competitive environment and, when offered the chance to advance me and increase my responsibility to additional markets, I resigned and resigned. I didn't know what I would do but I knew I didn't want to be in that position. The truth is I was unhappy.

There was never enough time to pursue my own hobbies since I had to leave home early in the morning, around five and would often not return until about seven in the evening. My husband (I was divorced and remarried) was also working a very busy job. So over the course of several years, we communicated via tiny notes left on our pillows and in the toilet bag and everywhere we could possibly surprise one another by writing a note of love. It was not a life. It was likely in these years that I began to doubt my choices, or lack of them and realized that there must be more to life than just going to work. I felt like the days were just disappearing between my fingers like the sand that floats in an hourglass that physically indicates that there's ever-shrinking time.

High-Income and Fast Cars and fancy Travels

As I was a employee who was unhappy with my job I was approached by a friend who was looking to introduce me to an intriguing business opportunity. The woman and another were in my kitchen for a while and created a picture for me, which I was ecstatic about. I could start my own business and travel all over the world, without any particular investment or financial risk and still have the security of a good income, fast cars , and extravagant travel. The most appealing thing about this was that it didn't take much effort - I only needed to bring some other people on board and we were off in the process of establishing. I would be completely free of any income and, being one of the very first to join Denmark I would be among the top of the line and earn a lot of money.

Wow! It almost sounded like it was too amazing to be true, however, since I had a good impression of the woman as an honest and trustworthy individual I was confident for a moment that she was telling the truth and it was an opportunity worth taking advantage of. In my mind I thought about whom I could contact and quickly came up with an imaginary list of about 10-12 acquaintances and friends whom I believed would purchase because they are interested with health issues and balanced diet.

The product did not attract me, but I found the business model appealing. I was unable to comprehend the nuances of the payment plan but I can always get acquainted with it in the future. So , I decided to purchase an entire beginner's kit and when I received it, ran out to my friends and acquaintances to promote the healthy supplements and have them recruit four of their acquaintances to join too. My intention wasn't that all my acquaintances would benefit from a super-healthy nutritional supplement to prevent various illnesses of the lifestyle. It was not that they could also earn an additional source of income. It was not the intention to make me wealthy quickly and gave little thought about the demands of a career in this business.

To my surprise and annoyance I was confronted with the words "No". Thank you, no. It's too costly. The best option is to consume vegetables and vitamins regularly. This is not an elaborate scheme. We don't have time for it. Then again, I can't afford it. It goes continue with the exact same reasoning. When I finally got the conclusion "No" at the ninth consecutive time I began to feel cold feet and believed that of course it was impossible to earn money in this manner. To be successful in this field, I would be the first to go, as the market was soon going to be flooded - the next thing you know? The truth is that this was an excuse to myself, since I was not been aware of what I was expected to know in order to be an expert networker. In my excitement I had leapt into the pool of opportunity - and received the kind of experiences that we will recognize - simply because I hadn't considered the possibility seriously.

I would like to stress how the business was two years ahead of its industry. The person who founded it is still employed by the company and is highly regarded and has seen it grow massively internationally, and has earned total revenue of around USD 85 million. Since when. Since then, it wouldn't be as if the company's products were of low quality and their business model and payment system had proved not to work as well. At that time, I didn't know what this meant and wasn't equipped to fully comprehend the issue. My mentor, the lady whom I introduced to the business likely didn't grasp the potential of the idea, considering I didn't receive any guidance. I went to sellmy products, then got lost and quit. Just like thousands of others in the present.

As I reflect to that time, my plan at the time left an extraordinary bad smell on my tongue. I recall that I was not going to consume these pills for my self ... Why do my peers approve of this plan? The biggest problem was that I wanted to be rich quickly, as I considered it to be my personal way to get rid of the job I hated. I was of the opinion that the concepts that underlie Network Marketing were smart but I wasn't sure to myself if it was too clever or if it was an element or a kind of pyramid scheme as a close friend had explained to me. Actually I was unsure what the entire "pyramid" idea was about. I'm not proud to consider the fact that personal success was the primary motive however, when I'm honest with myself, that is exactly what I was thinking about. This is among the reasons Network Marketing has been branded as a negative one. There have been too many quick, clever and superficial individuals who, like me, created a completely false image about Network Marketing.

Consultant for New Energy

As you've probably guessed I took the decision to resign to Philip Morris. Family and friends shook their heads, and they couldn't know how I could quit the status of a regular wage and a car. Without any job opportunities. How do I find an equally lucrative job if I didn't have a formal training? I think they were concerned for my sake.

However, I was relieved! It was like a great weight was taken off my shoulders, and I felt full of new energy.

I didn't want to be an employee once more. I was looking to become a self-employed which is why I signed various consulting deals with Danish brands that I introduced to the sector that my previous position had offered me a solid network. It was the perfect fit for me as the brand's owners were responsible for the entire cost of storage, production, and delivery which meant that my sole job was to market their products in exchange in exchange for a percentage. It was not in my nature for me to have the privilege of being "completely independent" and to fund the start-up of a business with everything involved and I was happy with the way the things went. There were no financial risks, there was no bosses, and no demands for management and administration responsibilities. This was the perfect kind of model for me.

Things were going well, and in a brief time frame, Kraft Jacobs Suchard, one of the subsidiaries from Philip Morris, offered me an agreement to freelance consult for Toblerone the world's top sought-after chocolate on the market for travel. I couldn't resist that invitation. In fact, it was precisely what I been looking forward to however, I saw a chance to earn some serious income while continuing to be having fun doing what I excelled in and enjoyed. The company was aware and understood that I didn't want to be a part-time employee and did not require any administrative work and I was aware that I could improve sales by winning more prominent product placements in stores. The pay was an excellent regular commission and an attractive and progressive bonus in the event that I went over my budget which is why I jumped into the job. After a couple of months, Toblerone had top placements all over the world, but it was then that the entire nature of the work changed. It was now necessary for the positions maintain their status. However, maintenance isn't my area of expertise. I'm creative and entrepreneurial And so, I became bored, and in spite of a very good income, I decided to end the deal. It was to me not about money but rather passion. I'd experienced some years when I was almost bursting with energy and enthusiasm and was thrilled to travel across the country in pursuit of my goals. It was enjoyable, and I was content. It was how I wanted to live my day and enjoy my time.

The higher you climb, the more you fall

Alongside this Toblerone agreement, I created a successful business using exclusive pashmina shawls that were made by myself in Nepal. I had 40 colors in stock and provided 70-80 shops across

Denmark, Norway and Sweden. An investment of a significant amount for me.

A family of 6 in Nepal were able to survive on the income that a self-employed salesman and me managed to bring up and running, so I was thrilled and proud at the same time. I was happy. I suddenly became becoming a "real" business owner and was able to contribute by providing honest work and earnings for fantastic people living in a developing nation which was where the most help I could provide was to create jobs. My partners' confidence grew, and their self-esteem increased and they purchased a motorbike and were planning to build homes in Kathmandu and I was extremely proud of the things I was able to contribute to. My family and friends considered me cool, and I appreciated their praise.

The whole thing was abruptly ended when a major supermarket chain celebrated its birthday . They it appeared on the front of its birthday catalog it offered Pashmina Shawls for sale at a cost which was less than my actual production cost. That stung! I don't know if anyone can picture the feeling that I felt in my stomach after I looked at the catalogue? It was like I was smashed right into the gut. I could barely breathe. In my mind, I knew I was back to square one , and that my wonderful friends would not be able to earn an income, and that I would myself suffer a massive financial loss.

I was correct. The phones stopped working every day until the next. There was no assistance that could be gotten at the retail - I was left to fend for myself with my stockpile as well as a new shipment scarves and shawls is on the on the way, and a new project in progress. I was tired and stressed but I was unable to sleep in the late at night. I was also embarrassed and my shame kept me from sharing my feelings, and I was basically by myself with my problems. My previous goal of having fun and feeling happy was replaced by financial worries and money.

My mother had taught her son to become a decent as well as a decent human being. I was unable to convince myself to leave behind the agreements I signed between my partners in business therefore I paid for everything that was initiated - and was at a at a crossroads. I was depressed I was angry with me for not having business acumen and my inability to make an analysis of the situation in the market and my inexperienced approach to having to serve my customers beyond what they were entitled to beyond. The constant supply in 40 shades was an absolute requirement in my mind. Self-recrimination was never going to have any value.

I was totally disabled for a number of years following this and my self-esteem suffered greatly in the aftermath. It was a very emotional period, as my self-image was shattered and I was incredibly sad. After being the woman who was successful who had everything under control, I was now feeling unrecognizable and had no meaning. A feeling that was not enough prompted me to hide behind an idea that will provide me with the opportunity to look inside myself - and discover my personal values.

Impassioned Jewelry Designer and in Red

I "played" the role of a jewelry designer for a while and was enthralled with the design process. I set up a tiny gallery in the north of Copenhagen and was convinced I was in the right place, because I was like four-year-old Jannie sitting there with the pearls and stones which were transformed into gorgeous jewelry. The place was like a universe entirely my own and it was beneficial to me because I could think about my life and what I truly desired when I was in the back of the room creating jewelry. It was open only on Thursdays Fridays, Saturdays, and Sundays as I didn't want to adhere to the normal hours of opening and have to employ permanent employees. Additionally, I required the freedom to travel and explore the world. I had a few regular customers who loved coming to the gallery, and they requested me to design the perfect piece of jewelry for them - something that nobody else could obtain. I found it to be quite enjoyable and exciting however I was a long way from being completely immersed. I wasn't even close. In terms of finances, I was living with my savings and the gallery wasn't in the black.

The truth is that I was afraid! I was scared and uncertain of my abilities and capabilities. I was scared to be completely committed but after a few months I finally admitted my own self that I didn't have the courage or desire to be self-employed. I in no way, would be putting my financial security at risk due to the fact that. The money wasn't an important factor in my motivation. In contrast I was not prepared to risk money in order to build an economically viable business.

I was completely shattered by the Pashmina experience. The idea of being working from Monday through Saturday was depressing as I wanted to be independent and be able manage my time. Absolutely never would I ever want to return to employment as my need to take the decision-making process in my own hands was not in line with the conditions of employees. Also, because we didn't have to depend on a regular income for me, I decided I should "retire". The drawers and cupboards were filled, so cash was not a priority for me, so I could spend all day hedonistic and do cooking and laundry, take walks in the woods together with Black Diamonds (Labradors) as well as paint, read and travel. I was elated and satisfied.

Then Network Marketing popped up in my life once more.

Chapter 6: The Mistakes To Avoid

Each business you're looking to pursue has risks as well as advantages, disadvantages and. It is important to make potential disadvantages nothing and achieve satisfaction. One method to achieve success when it comes to network marketing is stay clear of the most common mistakes that individuals make. The following information is the top 10 most frequent mistakes that people make as they begin their career in network marketing.

Don't take advice from the wrong People

There are many people you'll need to speak to prior to deciding to decide to go into the world of network marketing.

Your family and friends are people who are willing to give you suggestions and advice. However, before making decisions about what they've got to say, think about what they've learned.

Does anyone in your family or friend circle had an enterprise? Has anyone ever tried network marketing? What are their thoughts and how do they align with your own?

For instance an example, there was a college student who was looking to switch schools. She was worried about earning a living in the new place since she was not going to be able to find a job immediately. She also planned to be living away from the campus. She was thinking that signing up for Mary Kay might be the best option in order to make sure that some cash will be flowing to her.

After speaking to her family, she began to think about the task ahead. It would require a lot of work to establish a client database for the newly-established city.

There is no friends or family members who live in this new town to assist her. Students at colleges are living on a budget therefore the earnings from this group of people wouldn't be able to work. Additionally, it was the days before the internet was massive. Her efforts would include socializing, which is difficult to do when taking 16 credits per semester. Also, she is an introvert, which means that socializing isn't her habit.

In weighing the effort and time required in addition to the lack of an adequate support system, as well as her personal style, she knew that networking marketing wouldn't work for her. Family members helped to point this out.

Your friends and family may be able to assist in this way. Sometimes, negative perceptions regarding a particular situation can help you to see the truth.

This can help you to be successful where other people thought you wouldn't.

But, don't shut down the advice. Instead, take a moment to listen to it, think about it, and finally determine if the advice is something you should follow. Individuals who don't have a good understanding of network marketing could get an incorrect impression. They might believe it's fraudulent in all respects. They could also be wary of it, mainly because they've never owned a business before and don't like the idea of investing required.

Conducting research and speaking with the most qualified people is the best method to avoid this error.

The most appropriate people to speak to is people who have participated with network marketing. It is also advisable to speak with the people within the business, not only the person who is trying to get you signed up as well as other employees. It's true that it sounds fantastic when statistics are circulated. But, is the information only about the top-performing sellers or do you get an accurate picture of potential earnings?

The more you learn about and interact with those working in the field of network marketing and the more you know the details of the industry, its possibilities and the efforts required to be successful.

Don't Take Your Choice Seriously

How do you earn money? Do you have experience selling goods via cold calls or door-to door? Network marketing differs from restaurant, retail and other options for career advancement. It is possible to start quickly, and with minimal preparation. You can also work as a freelancer and flexible in terms of time slots.

It may give you the impression that you do not have to take seriously the work you do and the effort you put into your marketing efforts. It is far from the reality. You will have to devote more effort in network marketingthan you would in your normal job. Still, you need to be committed to your decision.

All of your determination, persistence organizational, and career abilities are essential to be successful. If you don't be serious about network marketing is the moment when you are making peanuts for the time and effort you put into.

If you want to take network marketing seriously it is necessary to be committed to making sales via the many avenues available to you. These include managing your website as well as social media marketing content marketing, as well as word-of-mouth sales. Each avenue you have to generate sales is one you should make use of even if it's engaging with a stranger at the grocery store when they ask you questions about your bag of goods.

In actuality, you'll receive a kit from the company that runs network marketing along with incentives to reach your sales goals. Sometimes , you will receive bags, purses pin, or any other display device that you can carry along. Phone cases can be distributed by some networks of marketing businesses. These cases are used as conversation starters.

Making the Wrong Network Marketing Company

There are a lot of networking marketing firms available. They have a long track record such as Avon, Mary Kay, and Doterra of offering high-quality products. Others aren't as transparent, and don't have the long track record to support their credibility.

It doesn't mean every one of them is bad. However, it does indicate that some do not have a clear explanation and may be trying to sell you an idea that isn't likely to be successful.

Your level of study you conduct will determine the success of your network marketing. If you don't thoroughly study the business, you may be losing money instead of earning it. Instead of putting yourself in this situation Here are some questions to consider when looking at an organization from a business standpoint:

1. What is the time span that business been operating for?

2. What is their plan for marketing? How do you market your products and what should you begin with and how much marketing is done?

3. If there is an affiliate component to the network i.e. the recruitment of members under your control What are the incentive programs? Are you rewarded when you achieve certain sales? Mary Kay used to provide an automobile to its sales representatives if they achieved an amount. The mark was used to sell products and also to recruit new members.

4. Are there any representatives in your region? How many are working in the same area? Is the market ripe for another company selling the same product?

5. Have you got a potential market that you could sell to even if there's too many companies selling similar products?

6. Have you heard of complaints? Better Business Bureau complaints? Are there any news stories about the firm? Do you think the news is mostly positive?

The answer to these questions will determine whether your venture is success. Businesses that try to conceal the truth or don't provide sufficient information in the beginning typically not giving the most effective chance.

If there are a lot of complaints against a business there could be problems. Every business is not perfect however, you don't have to put yourself in a position for failure due to bad choices you make.

Begining the Work in a way that is not appropriate Expectations

What are your goals? What are your objectives? It's normal to have goals. It is important, however, to plan. But, there are certain expectations that could cause you to abandon the project before you even begin.

Write down your objectives. This will help you understand what you'd like from your business.If yes you're on the right track however, you need realistic expectations.

Goals and benefits are a good way to begin and determine what the company can offer you. When you look at companies, ask yourself if this company share similar goals to yours? Are they able to provide a high-quality product that you are able to sell? Are there any advantages or goals you aren't able to achieve with the businesses which are on the top of your list?

The companies you choose to work with will not give you every benefit. They may not be able to however, if you are able to find a business that matches many of the benefits and objectives you've set you can be content. As with any profession or job that you pick, there will be disadvantages. So long as you understand the downsides of your chosen career You can set realistic expectations.

The most important thing that individuals fail to address when they evaluate a company and determining their objectives is the amount of income they will generate through the network marketing firm they've chosen.

Many businesses try to attract you by promising you the best sales forecasts. However, it is important to be aware of the time and effort it takes to meet those targets. It's not an easy undertaking. It is not something that happens in a single day. It is possible that you're not able to reach your most important sales goals, or perhaps there won't be enough earnings generated from your business for other reasons.

The internet is a source of half-truths and inaccurate information. Certain companies require you to be enthusiastic, and you'll join as a network marketing professional. They will share with you the tales of success of buying an all-new car valued at $20,000. Their sales representatives earning $50,000 per year but they do not reveal that they are just 1% of marketers within the business. The majority of their customers do not ever get the brand new car, or even more than $10,000 annually in the event that they do.

The effort you're willing to invest in the network marketing business will decide the amount you'll actually make. If you only host one event every month, and you have two out of five guests buying every day it is unlikely to earn more than the sum of a few hundred dollars.

Realistic expectations demand that you make a commitment to the profession for more than just a modest income, if you've got the desire of earning an acceptable, full-time, income.

Selecting Business Partners in the Wrong Way

Network marketing does use a team. There are teams within each one of these cities that were enlisted by one person. In the event that you've got business associates who refuse for them to stop or sell due to the fact that they're not earning enough money, it will affect your motivations, and consequently your bottom number. You should be confident in the business you work for as well as the individuals who recruit you or who are being hired by you.

Failure to Remain afloat without proper effort

It seems that effort always return to effort. However, in fact that when you put more energy and effort invest in your marketing strategies for network marketing, the more you earn. If you're not putting in efforts to make yourself known to new customers, you'll not make much. Sure, it's good to earn discounts and maybe earn some money every now and then but if you truly intend to make money from a network marketing business, you have to invest the time and effort.

1. Make a decision based on thorough study.

2. Make sure you pay the initial costs of the kits and the website If one exists.

3. If you do not have a website, sign-up to create one and then make your own. It is also possible to use social media platforms instead of having a separate website hosted.

4. Start following people on social media.

5. Tell your friends and family be aware that you are a company representative.

6. Begin hosting events with people you love.

7. Spread the word about the fact that you're selling your products at these events and on social media.

8. Continue to repeat the process until eventually you will achieve the stability you need.

If you don't continue telling family members, friends and colleagues that you sell certain products that you'll lose customers. Keep in mind that customer retention is all about keeping your brand on the minds of consumers. The more work you put into it your efforts, the more you'll be recognized.

Incorrectly calculating time, effort, and ROI

The subject of the need for effort has been addressed. Make sure that when you think about the network marketing firm you're going to select to consider the time and effort involved when you calculate your calculations on return on investment. There are three aspects you should know about the potential of a business's earnings to determine the ROI on investment.

1. What is the cost of this starter kit?

2. How many items do you require to have on hand?

3. What's your time worth to you?

Most likely, you're working an active full-time job. What is your pay or hourly rate? Do you think the amount you earn is worth what you earn? Someone in their 60s with many years of experience in the field of caregiving is paid $11.50 per hour, but the same person could create their own and operate a home care service earning $20 or more per hour due to their experience. A person selling books might earn between $8 and $12 an hour, while the manager can earn an average of $13 to $15 per hour. The reason is that salaries are determined based on the experience of the employee and the affordability.

You might think that your experience and capabilities are worth 20 dollars per hour but do you really earn that amount through network marketing. No. You're more likely to earn minimum wage from network marketing, if you think about how much time that you will need spend marketing the products, attending parties, and selling items.

If you believe you deserve an increase in pay but you don't think the value of putting your time on network marketing. If you're confident you've got an established, reliable customer base prior to when you start network marketing it is possible to estimate a bit more value of your time. In the end, if you're currently dissatisfied about what your time might be worth, it'll be difficult to maintain your efforts. This can impact the ROI of your investment.

The ROI isn't just a matter in terms of duration, it is also rather the amount of money you need to invest to the kit. The process of earning $100 to purchase the kit could be as easy as having one celebration. It is usually. But, if you're not provided with a free website to establish, you must calculate the cost of establishing your site along with other advertising and marketing options you can choose to take.

At the conclusion of the day, If you approach network marketing with an open mind and with the appropriate mental state to put in the effort to put into your work and succeed, you will be successful. It is highly likely to be an extremely successful salesperson, provided that you have realistic expectations and you are putting your efforts into it. When you start to realize that you're more valuable than the effort you can yield it is when you'll commit a blunder.

Do not do this and you will succeed in the field of network marketing. You can do it.

Chapter 7: Strategies To Growing Your Business

Let's take a look at some strategies that help you earn profits and establish your business fast.

Recruitment is an important element

Being able to build a strong network of friends, family and others who are searching for opportunities might not help your position in the network. The most effective method to recruit is to consider looking at experts who have MLM experience . They could be involved in the products you choose to use or could be from an entirely different line of products. It is possible to continue and find distributors already part of the MLM program. The general scenario for the MLM system is the majority of them will give greater than 100 percent. However, they might not be able to earn the amount they had hoped for.

Therefore, if you are able to describe your program and advantages in the most authentic manner and take the time to appreciate their previous and present efforts They may actually begin doing work for you. Create an opportunity that is so thrilling that they consider you to be the most genuine individual they've ever met. If they notice the trust factor growing they'll refer lots of people to become part of your organization and network.

The Upline's weight

The Upline component in MLM is used to refer to those who are higher than you within the network. You must determine whether they're too heavy and don't do anything other than relying heavily on you to finish the task. One way to determine how useful they are to see the frequency of their calls to you, if they are attending meetings with you, and can they be helpful at the planning stage.

If you're new to the network, it's advised to establish a relationship with an upline or distributor person in the network that is experiencing great success in the manner they had envisioned. A whole new confidence level is evident when you talk to those you know already. This makes the explanation of the new product much more straightforward when compared to other groups all together. In addition, by observing the way your upline distributors communicate opportunities to other distributors You may pick up the best practices and implement these when it's your time.

The Downline benefit

There's no time. You have to wear so many hats that sometimes, attracting the right people isn't always the only task on which you must concentrate on. The first step to do when you bring someone into the network is to create an appropriate training plan for them. While you are doing this, you will need to concentrate on subtle aspects, such as encouraging them, supporting them in times of need and most importantly, being part of their "why" questions prior to them going alone. A rough estimate of time could be anywhere from four weeks before they leave to their own. Your ultimate goal is to ensure that new employees do not solely learn from you, but while learning, they develop long-lasting friendships with you and other members within the network.

Social media and the Internet

It is typically a plan which is a part of building your downline quickly. Social media and the Internet are now effective tools to grow your business quickly. The tips below are not new, but they provide the correct way to do things.

Pay per click Pay per click is one of the most reliable and well-known ways to earn money from MLM by using the internet is to the pay-per-click. It's easy, each click made by someone who clicks on an advertisement, site or blog post, the creator of the website or blog will be compensated in the exact same amount. When your plan is approved and you can run the content for a certain timeperiod, you'll begin receiving clicks. You will determine where you stand with respect to the possibilities that are available to you.

There are many websites you can use simultaneously to place your ads and gain leads. If you strike the perfect chord and you can make it a profit with your campaign, you can shift to the next quickly to gain many more leads. The only downside is that you will need to spend some money to have your ads run elsewhere and should a mistake occur during this time may not have enough or even no time to correct it.

Blogging: The most effective way to make use of your blog and increase traffic is to making sure that your blog visitors are educated with your site. Because the topic of discussion is one that is connected to networking marketing, your goal is to provide regular suggestions, tips about trends, new the latest trends, best practices and do's as well as some appealing headings for your blog, like "how to make money and grow your network quickly'. The most significant benefit you can enjoy with blogging is that it's solely yours and no one could claim to be responsible for what you have written (as as long as it's unique content). Blogs are referred to as long-term - after they have been established and the traffic begins to come in it will keep running year after year for as long as you create relevant and interesting articles. You must ensure that the content you write is beneficial to anyone who truly would like to be successful in MLM. In writing, you must not be too general and only highlight specific topics. However, you need to ensure that you provide certain important details for them. This is the reason they will be inclined to revisit your website or blog. The benefits of blogging are numerous ways. One such is that it requires a minimum time to establish and requires little or no funds to set up a blog.

It can also be slow in the event that you don't concentrate on linking and create your blog in order to get it noticed quickly. It sometimes is more time-consuming to study a specific area and then write about the subject to create a beautiful appearance. If you're starting your blog for the first time, it's going to be a long process and therefore it is essential to check out websites that offer online assistance and that make it easy to set up.

Marketing via videos is an effective method to reach your audience since they contain both video and audio that can help build the desired confidence. The audience can sense the authenticity when you address a subject that's be the most emotional component of what they're looking for. Your voice and body language must be confident and convince the person to believe in what you are saying. Videos, unlike blogging, are more effective, because they are able to feel emotions, laughter and can keep them entertained throughout. The only thing you have to do is let go of your fear of speaking to cameras.

Targeted or Solo ads It is a good idea in the event that you are able to identify who you can use. Solo ads are those that an influencer has number of followers via email, which is usually massive and you pay the influencer or group to send emails on behalf of you. Although there is some cost associated with it but it's considered to be the most efficient method of reaching your intended people. If properly targeted this approach could be extremely effective since it can bring in more leads in a shorter period of time. It does not require any technical knowledge to carry out it. The only thing to be looked after is the way people read these emails.

Today, each email goes to spam folders, and some emails are automatically pushed to the spam folders or are classified as scams. It all comes down to the way you write a subject line with a heading to ensure that your email doesn't end up to spam, and then pay an attention to the content to ensure that it isn't perceived as a fraud. There are many more information on subject lines and information from the web when you browse.

Websites for social media there is a certain belief that only the most popular social media websites can draw visitors, and that having an account on these websites will bring you a lot of leads. The other line of thought is that every social media site will still be able to find your content via SEO if you are aware of the rules of play. You can explore more on the web or get more information from your SEO contacts who may be of assistance.

One option is to get accounts on these sites and then purchase ads on these sites which have pages that are popular. The most significant benefit social media websites have is their 'reach'. This makes them one of the most sought-after and easy strategies to assist you in building your networks. The only downside is that you don't have the website since you only have an account and a few visitors that will check out the content you've got.

Concentrating on numbers

The standard understanding of the MLM system is that you must find 3 people, which in turn will get three per. The most difficult thing that you face is trying to figure out who's exactly similar to you. The majority of the efforts you put into your work should be identical to those made by those who are similar to you. The job isn't over even if you've enlisted 3 new members in your network. The issue is how massive the number of people you can recruit and the higher the number, the greater. You can't expect every distributor will behave what you would like to.

Therefore, if you hire distributors from 100s, it is possible that you'll get a fair percentage of them who are working to build the network.

While your focus is on quantity of distributors you choose to appoint one of the best ways to evaluate your options is to keep track of those who are able to duplicate your efforts. If, for example, you've recruited 500 distributors over the course of five years, and the 480, 480 have done very little, due to reasons that are not clear Your chain might remain viable with the 20 who are working towards the end target. The 20 over a long time period can help bring over 25000 distributors in the network.

It is crucial to understand that your the focus should be on a select few distributors, with your aim is to find more more distributors. While doing this ensure that this information is shared with your downline on a regular basis. The majority of MLM millionaires and entrepreneurs who made it realize that it's all about managing numbers and playing around with them to achieve success with network marketing.

Who do you want to target

Your goal is to be successful, which is natural to discuss your opportunities with successful and positive people. Additionally, if are able to instill this mindset to your team members, then quickly your network will be extremely engaged and will produce results that would be unheard of. If you believe that successful people are constantly busy with multiple commitments, you're destroying the idea of focusing on them before you try this approach.

The secret lies in the fact that most of the people who are successful are able to demonstrate a high degree of openness and understanding, and they are always prepared to take in new ideas and concepts. They recognize that the most crucial thing for success is having a listening ear and a compassionate attitude. If you're new to the world of networking, the most important rule to be followed is to ensure that you don't spend too much time with those who are simply prospects but with no results (yes or not). They are usually close friends, family members and relatives who look at the opportunities but don't do anything about it.

Therefore, the rule of thumb is to not waste one second with prospects who do not have any motivation. It is believed among the best-performing individuals within the MLM that five highly motivated distributors in your network could be able to eliminate 1000 prospects who are negative.

Pay attention and be sure to answer clearly

If you are focused on promoting your business, you might miss prospects who have something to say. It is widely known that you have to find more distributors , and in order to do this it is necessary to speak to many people. When you are doing this however, you must also possess patience and time to pay attention to what every prospect is saying. You should also ask them the appropriate questions to find out what their goals are and why they'd prefer to consider network marketing as a way to make money.

Once you've gathered the right information, it is easy to help them navigate the procedure and turn to a successful recruits. Therefore, the more you pay attention to your prospects, they have better chances of becoming part of your network. When you can assist to establish their priorities, and then help the daily and weekly plan and then you've made a fortune that will make money by following a defined strategy.

If you've got a new chance and you are interested, you must consider what the best option is for you. You can show them the best possibilities and guide them through several attractive presentations however, as long as they believe they can figure it all on their own, you , or they're unable to take a step forward.

If you are considering offering the chance to offer it to someone else, you must first be convinced that it's possible and that nothing will keep you from achieving it. To do this should you be required to study some information or get some training, complete it and then carry your steps forward.

Infusing culture is the environment you serve

You are the head of your group in the context of your downline. Anything you speak or write should be embedded within your downline. Any company or business you represent has an established culture. It is your obligation to ensure that the culture is appreciated, accepted and respected by all applicants. Even if your recruitment doesn't prove to be successful, you must insist that the company's culture is explained in the form of by word of mouth.

Certain companies ensure that they have regular meetings with their distributors frequently and distributors too have a tendency to make it a habit to visit their networkers regularly since they form bonds. The culture can be instilled by many different ways, and especially in the field of network marketing, everyone is with the goal of making cash quickly and improving their lives along the way. In order to keep your team cohesive and productive, strive to connect the team together through a common culture that is in close connection with the corporate's lifestyle that is in line with the person's lifestyle.

Finally, success in the long-term is contingent on how the person in the network works hard to develop the business over a long period of time. As everyone knows, the development and the results occur with a consistent effort for two or more years, it is vital that the person stays to the organization for that time.

Rewarding and appreciating

Everybody joins in with a sense of conviction or simply the belief that they will get towards their goal. However, it is a challenge to sustain this enthusiasm and inspire them to reach the top level. It might be in fragments that you recognize and thank the effort of your employees, but it's everything that is important is.

When you're planning your next presentation, ensure you invite these brand new distributors and assign them a an important role. Since they're new and need to be noticed fast, they are awed by recognition which will be the greatest incentive for them. It is essential to identify with everyone the things that make them happy, and include those phrases and words during public meetings. This will surely bring them joy and they will begin to believe that you are at the correct spot. They'll be keen to grab the chance quickly and succeed.

Everyone to do everything

There is nothing that can replace you other than yourself. Your ideas and actions could be replicated , but at the end the day, everyone must take on the challenge of wearing multiple roles to be able to interact with the most people they are able to. The hats you wear can be anything from a leader, coach and student to teacher or worker to an employer and a the thinker, to that of a dreamer. In the workplace when you need to ascend the corporate ladder, you must to let a few people down and then climb the ladder by proving your skills. When it comes to network marketing, you must help all and include them when you need to climb the ladder.

Generating wealth and cash flow

Every person will experience the cash-strapped situation at some moment or the other. The most frequent situations are the accumulation of credit card debt at the end of the month , and massive loan payments. At the end of the month, the funds are exhausted before the necessary payments are completed. This means that the majority of them end up going from hand to mouth and accumulating enormous debts over the course of time. In the end it is likely that they won't be able to contemplate their dreams and goals.

This is especially true especially if you come from a family with a low income since your debts will likely to mount and eventually become an unending story. Then you begin dreaming of being rich overnight, or search for a place that will let money fall into your lap.

In the event of an income stream that is positive, the scenario will be in the opposite direction of what was described earlier. In these kinds of circumstances, your income will be higher than the monthly expenses. Network marketing can be the solution to this. It allows a person to be in control of their thoughts and control over his or her destiny and make things happen in their own manner. These risks in relation to investments and time is minimal in comparison to other area you might want to think about.

The only area that can allow for exponential growth is in network marketing. Once you're on the right track, your cash flow is positive and surpasses your expenses, and the excess money can then be used for opportunities similar to those.

Chapter 8: Disciplined Thoughts

The fact that the core team was assembled was one thing. It was now about HOW, what to do to turn the situation around. We all had a clear list of problems and now was the time to get the right strategy.

At this moment I wasn't focused on status, but rather to stay above the water.

It was about settling with the present moment not yesterday, and not basing too heavily on a vision of the future when something was never even happening.

I didn't wish to be great at first, only to remain in the glory days from the past. I wanted my team to be a strong, firmly embedded values and a culture in which every aspect can be changed whether it's technology or the environments, however the core values and the culture will never change.

This was the beginning of the difficult task of aligning our thoughtsand attitudes and beliefs to create an idealized culture that everyone can accept and strive towards. This was not about having a culture that was ruthless but rather having a strict discipline in order to emerge from this state.

What type of culture are we looking for? A team culture, a selfish one or a distinctive culture?

This was the question that was on the table to be asked at the moment.

Truth is better than dreaming

Customers didn't want cheaper prices, they wanted a higher kind of product

The intention was to create a dream that was significant, emerging of the deep waters and from the deep hole that is to say However, there was there was one thing that it was not and it wasn't about one man's redemption, or one man's glory. Once I go down, the empire will fall with me.

It was about creating an everlasting empire and a culture that endures. any successor who takes over shares identical values, and values and that run through their veins.

Although it was easy to say it was going to be a lot of work to get the job completed

I began by asking questions and confronting the facts. I met with the nine Members of the Core and asked them these questions, which were passed around by 13 of them.

Where are we at the moment?

How terrible is it?

Who's currently on the bus?

Are they sitting in the right seat?

Can we save it?

Do we have the ability to turn it around?

Do we still have faith in our business?

Do we believe that we're networkers?

Do we have an unrealistic idea of being meaningful?

We're significant because we realise that we've got a problem to conquer , as do other people, whom we assist in conquering their own.

What were we going to do? achieve this?

The brutal truths exposed allowed us to concentrate on the issues that was at hand, and not get distracted by other, less important priority issues.

Believe in yourself

This chapter was composed shortly after I was at my son's ceremony to rebrand for his school.

What a great idea, having a discussion about the future with my colleagues and taking part in a celebration to mark the occasion.

It's known as "synchronicity"

The head of the school stated that after 16 years at an education that was at the top of its game,, it was time to adapt to technology, yet still hold on to our beliefs and values.

The rest will be different, but we're still at the top of the line in education. This was awe-inspiring and very the first time I have heard my Thoughts. And I am confident it will rise to impressive heights. I am so happy for my son to be going to a school like this. To that end often, it has happened to me that I came up with new ideas , and be able to come up with amazing thoughts only to have them snubbed by a remark stating:"you don't have the right age" as well as "has your system been proven before?"

How can it be proven itself if you don't give me the chance to demonstrate it.

This was also the case with some of the up-lines, believing they've been in the field, they have the insider knowledge and that only what they have to say is to be followed and other information should be left out.

I was able to recall creating an Excel spreadsheet to assist the team with adding names and funnel systems from my corporate world to display the condition of the prospect

It was a good way to determine if it was worth pursuing the opportunity, close the deal immediately, or make a plan to meet at a later date.

However, due in the system not ever being utilized in the past, it was rejected by the upline, and the team would listen to the upline since after all, if you look at Nandish who could to come in with an idea?

However, if it comes from the great upline and we agree, then we do our gracious acceptance.

A perception I wanted to alter, a sense of humility, a willingness to listen to other people and be aware of the best time to implement an concept at just the right moment.

Trust in your efforts and believe that you've tried and you know the results. It will only improve your leadership abilities and remember to share it with others.

I've tried this, and I've tried this and that. That's what the significance of it is all about: Learning from experiences sharing it, and then growing from it, but not absconding from it and applying it to the creation of an impressive empire.

It is reminiscent of a quote by Fred Pirdue, executive of "Pitney Bowes" in which he stated: "When you turn over the rock and take a look at the squiggly things beneath You can put the rock back down or say, "My task is to turn tocks and take a look at the squiggly objects regardless of the things you see could be terrifying to you"

In the face of the harsh facts, the question was:"what ways can we get the team to show their true colors without focusing on me instead, but at us, and on the task ahead?"

The book "Good to Excellent" in the book "Good to Great" by Jim Collins mentioned four of that I was familiar with and still frequently use:

1. A climate in which the truth is acknowledged

In addressing the tough questions above, during the initial creation of the team exposed was vital.

To tackle the little things, we'd not spend much time discussing our modest success but dedicate time to understand the road map to the goal we want to achieve, significance.

The fact that was accepted to all of us is that we're here to complete an obligation and be able to communicate our thoughts and opinions in a manner that is accepted, debate and accept it.

The environment that was created was known as trespass. The term itself refers to the act of being able to enter another property without permission. However, in this instance it was done with permission.

In this way , one could be confident to listen to matters that were delicate, near to the heart, yet needed to be addressed.

When a leader lets himself to be the sole fact rather than the situation that is at hand, can lead to failure.

There was a time when I was thinking that I could being the tough boss of the Italian mafia and everybody should follow my advice. We only be aware of what has is happening to the mafia today to understand why this approach is not working.

2. Create an environment that is conducive to people can hear the truth.

The question was "How do I get people to be motivated by presenting Brutal facts when the picture is so definable and set for disaster? Do you think it is better to talk about the good days ahead that can inspire the group?

No!

Whatever amount of flattery you use sweet words, they will not remove the sting beneath.

To grow, you must take care of the wound first. to heal the wound , we need to confront the truth what is the depth? I needed to know that my team is not built on Ego but rather through an act of trespass.

How do you create a culture where the truth can be being heard?

Answer questions, not the answers!

I had an issue when I was asked to present my opinion without always realizing that I was wasting my time discussing something that wasn't really relevant.

I began to train me to take my time, be attentive, asking more specific questions, but not to rephrase the questions.

Smart questions yield smart answers.

Sometimes, I noticed some of the members on the team who are looking at the tough man to be a bit hesitant to ask questions in order to avoid getting put in the bad books of the other members.

This is a sign of vulnerability and weakness. You'll need to overcome to become capable of overcoming.

I was often asking questions such as Do you feel satisfied by the results this week? And If not, why?

What is the best way to do it?

In group meetings or during training I'd begin with questions. When other people respond, it is a sign that they're committed to the task at hand.

I'd like to question their mindset, "is this right, do you recognize the leader within you? Is this the most you can do"

I was doing research on their personal development because I wanted generals, not puppets.

The questions weren't aimed to put the team, core members or anyone else down, but rather to gain an understanding of the circumstances.

3. Do not make a mistake in your conversation.

My new core team became more than just a thinking tank, but my family that understood my attitude and behavior.

However, we do occasionally engage in a rage Of course we do but it's normal for an enlightened team. I remember a time when I was tempted to beat my teammate

I know, the angry young man however, it was part of learning curve.

Humility isn't just a theoretical concept but also practical.

The environment became one in which we debated, discussed and then implement ideas, and at the same time , allow us to hear what others think of as our flaws.

4. Okay, here's the corpse Who did it? Conduct autopsies without the blame.

In the very early days , when I first started network in the year 2004, during the time of 2005/2006, there were the first 16 core members. God knows how this was managed , but it was chaotic and some members quit because of pressure or shut out, and as a result 13 members remained and it's an example that I am sharing.

I am not ashamed of my mistakes and I've made plenty of them, from relationships to not being a procrastinator.

While many people do not want to discuss the errors they made, according to their own experience, it can make them feel less than.

It was therapeutic to discuss it, debate it and inform others in the hope that they take the lessons learned and not repeat the same mistakes. I have learned that we all have to be accountable to our choices.

Take a look in the mirror and make a point at the person who is not that you can blame other people.

Start by being yourself.

I wanted to understand what my problem was I was a part of it and If so, what could I do to help improve my own self

Problems will not disappear, they'll reappeared until the lesson has been understood

I wanted to be able to communicate with others, including my own thoughts about where I am and how I am doing, and the team had to look at the situation and listen to others in the spirit of growing and not negative

5. Are you able to see your red flag? Create red flag mechanisms!

What systems do your organization have to demonstrate the performance of your company?

Do you see the financial result as being a red signal and inquire about the reasons?

Are you using the Excel or Word document that you need to fill each week to show your progress?

The red flag mechanism designed for the team was "A.S.K"

Attitude

Skills

Knowledge

What attitude did you take to the current situation you encountered with regard to your business?

What are the techniques you employed to achieve results? did you solicit, invite and sign-ups you already have?

What new knowledge did you acquire today? What book did you discover today that you can share?

The techniques were developed to aid in achieving goals. When there are no results it was time to ask what caused this to happen. The team was able to gain a better understanding of the way they're developing and what the red flags lie.

The system was able to help to create an illustration, so that we can see how far we've come.

It also prevented us from talking about unnecessary things, and instead focused on facts that were drawn up or sketched on paper.

The facts were clear and we had to comprehend what needed to be accomplished. It was like the checklist.

Our attitude toward fear and ideas is based on our fear of change and

Our capabilities are constantly improving our presentation skills through our presentations as well as our personal growth

Our expertise in staying current with the most recent developments and information.

Faith in the brutal realities

Everyone has a seed for excellence, goodness and importance in them, the difference is which one that you feed, water or cultivate.

Every person has been on a journey. The reason I can remember, the end of the expansion of the business was due to the fact that it was the time not permitted to employ its own ideas which were derived from within the organization, and always paying attention to concepts from other countries that were that were not appropriate to our current the market, or scenario.

There was a time when other teams that were rising, showing signs of growth and traits of effective leaders.

We were frequently pitted against them, even if they did not get their complaints addressed by saying, look at how these teams are performing very well, and then take a look at your team completely soiled.

It was painful however, in a way we looked at it as if the wheel is not always in the right direction and moving upwards, we had to do things in a consistent manner and always believe that we have the answer to creating the momentum.

The best part about it wasthat there was a goal that we could look at, take a step towards, push ourselves to the next level, and unleash our creativity into the team and be focused on the goal of getting there.

I can recall that during that period, my mother being an old-fashioned Hindu woman, was convinced that there was deeper to my death, and wanted to seek advice from spiritual people or a Swami. I'm not sure whether they earn money off of it or if they really are honest about what is going on. At the time, I was willing to do anything. So I went along just to listen to the obvious.

The swami said: "I see darkness all over my son. Roads are blocked. People are at a loss, they've done things and it's going be very difficult to overcome this" This is the final thing I would like to hear?

And I was thinking: "what is the solution Swami?""Prayers my son, your prayers and prayers alone will get you get through it"

He said something toward the final part of the discussion: "Pray son, but continue doing what you're supposed to do" Then I thought to myself whether I should change the way I conduct myself in order to make it work for me, or will appear as if I'm being a fugitive.

It took me a long time and deep reflections to arrive at my unwavering faith in God and resolve to be adamant in knowing when there is something wrong, but believing that it will work and be successful.

Do I trust in the vehicle? The answer was Yes. I believe in the vehicle, specifically network marketing. I am that the model is a method of escape and to help me reach my goals and get over my suffering. In the midst of the noise, I was able to hear and, let me tell you it felt like the darkest time of my life.

I took a conscious choice that my determination to reach the best is my main goal. Prayers certainly helped me to strengthen my determination and help me keep my mind focused and focused.

Meditation every morning helped me to keep my commitment to accomplish it.

When I first was aware that some people were against me. I was very angry but I also learned that the more people in my way or were disapproving of me could result in the same issue, "damn I am good so go ahead and that's all you've received. There is a lot more to do to stop me. It helped me to be more resilient. It could take time, but I will emerge and win."

As I was recalling the experiences while writing this, I was having it awful, my marriage was failing as well as a car I had to return as well as land assets. I was losing everything before my eyes.

A small voice inside my head was saying: "Nandish, you and I have a buddy, we are will make it happen but when I'm not sure but I know is that we'll"

Was I meant to be a failure and play short? Absolutely not! The team was not either despite the critics We were bound to rise to the top, eventually becoming significant. I didn't want to simply restructure my life, but allowed me to build something larger and stronger.

EGATES Mon Kapave, NouKapve Literally stating that EGATES, I CAN WE CAN, WE ARE EGATES.

The Stockdale Paradox

As I sat in the midst of aware of the Brutal facts and having the confidence and determination to solve the issue. I asked myself why some people quit when everyone was convinced on the road toward significance, towards financial freedom. It was then that I realized, how it was written in the publication "Good to Excellent" explained it that the optimists were the ones who had to quit first and failed to make it.

They were the ones who would say, this is the year that is coming up and this is the time that we're going to receive our checks and I'm going to expand and the time passed and nothing would happen or anything so they began to lose faith and settling for instant gratification without addressing the stark realities of our time and the fact that we were in a puddle , a deep one, and it was not about tomorrow, today however, having confidence that at in the day will come when we'll win.

Chapter 9: Promotion Of The Events

What's an Event?

In order to be successful in the field of network marketing, you need to master the art of promoting events. Many people do not realize the importance of events, and their businesses suffer for it. To understand the significance of events, you must know what is considered as an event.

An event could be any kind of conference call or presentation, training event or gathering of employees that are larger than you. Events let potential customers see more of the business and also the potential.

Why should you promote events?

One of the main reasons to advertise events is to provide people with an opportunity to view the larger view. If they visit in a room with just your rep and another they aren't aware of how huge the potential is. They don't understand how much impact this business has had on the lives of many other individuals.

They may not yet know what the company can offer them, so it is essential to convince them to go to an event. The best method to get people to go is to advertise the event.

How to Promote Events

Understanding how to market events is essential to the success of a Network Marketing career. One of the most important aspects of promoting events is to use "fear of losing." Remember that people always choose to be more concerned with the stakes they are taking than what they stand to gain.

Include statements like "This is only a once occasion to meet ...", "I do not know when the next event similar to the one you attended", "I'm not even sure if I can make it onto your guestlist." It is essential to create an event that is worth the attendees' time by promoting it and sounding as if it's a once every-so-several-year opportunity.

If you want to be successful with Network Marketing, you must attempt this. Top earners in this list are master marketers.

Learn to teach your team how to Promote Events

After you've learned to organize events, it is important to instruct your team members in how to market events. It's not enough that are the sole one to promote. It is also essential to train your team members to follow suit; it's the only way to generate massive momentum for your company. Train your team on the ability to overcome fear of loss as well as words that motivate people to take action.

Ask them to use phrases like "One only once special event", "I only have two VIP seats left", "Only a select number of guests are included on the list of guests." They are the kinds of phrases that can cause people to alter their plans, make commitments to attend, and then attend.

There is a well-known quote from the Network Marketing world that is, "One meeting must lead to another!"

When you attempt to connect with the prospective by way of phone calls or webinars, your goal does not aim to sign someone to a contract or offer an item, but to engage the person you're talking to to be engaged in the conversation.

Many Network marketers have made a splash when they figured out how to get this principle to work within their system. They made a lot of cash during the process. The trick is to engage the potential customer with your proposal until the prospect will accept to come back for another meeting.

To increase the success of the Network Marketing business farther and greater, you have to learn an essential skill that is business promotion!

If there's a skill that the top performers are able to master It is promotion. They are aware that the goal is to get people to attend their next event, they need to take action to ensure that people are eager to attend the next event.

To aid you in mastering this art We offer some suggestions to try and test before promoting events in the near future.

1. You shouldn't expect anyone else to be informed about what's going on when your team doesn't have even the slightest clue about the same. Make sure you communicate every detail with your staff.

It is also important for you to understand that a random email does not suffice to communicate. You should communicate your ideas on a one-to one basis, and when necessary, via the phone.

2. You are aware that the you need to inform your team Also, be aware that all team members must be engaged. Participating in the team ensures that each takes the event as their own or her own, and works together to make it an event that is successful. The more you can have, the more fun!

3. In order to keep contact between your team members make sure to send updates to them every day.

4. Create team events that are games that will set the tone for collective responsibility and gains for the whole team.

5. Don't go all-out to host a huge event. It is better to organize small events and ultimately lead to the main event. This way you'll be able to create an abundance of enthusiasm in the crowd, while chatting with them on the reasons the reasons they should attend the big event in a fun manner.

6. Given the anxiety that comes with organising an event of this magnitude it's easy to get depressed and your level of energy can drop. Do not let these thoughts influence your.

7. It is essential to maintain health good.

Chapter 10: Network Marketing Tips, Strategies And Tricks That Work

Every business will succeed if the proprietor is willing to learn the techniques, tricks and strategies to get the results he's trying to achieve. The business of networking marketing isn't special. There are obvious guidelines to get you clients from any company, like making decisions quickly or being an authority in your own company or building a list customers that you can be able to count on. There are also techniques, tricks and strategies that are specific to each kind of business and they are the ones that you must be seeking out to be successful with internet marketing. Here are some tricks techniques, tips and strategies to get you starting with network marketing:

Make yourself aware of the subject.

Network marketing can be a challenging process, and can be a daunting task for someone who isn't a pro at the actual business. To get started with the right foundation and succeed in this type of enterprise, you have to make sure you've got a solid understanding of the subject up your sleeves. You can find MLM scams everywhere on the internet and numerous people are falling for these traps, without even realizing they were falling for it. Knowing the facts will help you stay away from these scams and make sure that you're running your business in a safe and secure manner. Be aware that the more you are aware about your business, the better you'll be able defend yourself from scammers as well as scammers and the better you'll be able to develop the right strategy to succeed.

Utilization of PR to raise awareness

Word of mouth is the most effective strategy for marketing to get your product into the hands of people who may have an interest in your products. How can they find out the benefits of your product and what it can do for them? In the past marketers relied on word of mouth to create their network marketing programs, but with the advances in computer technology it's very simple to get the word out to many potential customers. This can be done by a variety of methods including through the making use of blogs. You can use bloggers to reviewyour products and company, with agreatcall-for-action which willgetthe readers inquiring more aboutthe companyandtheproducts.

Make sure you mention people who have an impact on your business

These are business professionals who have already made a profit in their business. What you are trying to achieve with this is to establish credibility and demonstrate to the potential clients your experience. It's good for business when you surround yourself with people who are successful with a strong reputation in the marketplace. people will be able to identify you with an experienced businessperson and are more likely to express their enthusiasm for your company, because they now be confident in them. A lot of successful businesspeople have excellent follow-up that wait for the chance to get to know the big name. This is the opportunity you'll be giving those who connect your business with a specific influential person in their field of.

Utilization of social media

There are social media platforms that are designed specifically for network marketers. These are the sites which you should join to get more information about network marketing and connect with people in similar interests with you. IBO Toolbox is a popular social media site used by network marketers across the globe. On the toolbox, you'll discover a lot, including various ways you can market your company and strategies you can employ to increase your reach. It is also possible to create a network marketing strategy that is more popular by using these platforms. This will attract customers to join your network for success over the long term.

Find out how to get the right customers

A lot of time could be wasted if you begin pitching your idea to every people that you meet and even those who have no desire to join a network marketing. It's much easier to do this if you have those who have an interest in network marketing and the money to invest in this kinds of businesses. People are searching for all sorts of information online today which is why this platform should be the channel you need to use to reach out to those that are looking for the services you have to offer. Pick the best search terms to find users online, for example such as join buy distributor, purchase discount, order and other like terms that are commonly employed in network marketing.

Pick a company that offers products you enjoy-

Every business will be successful if the person who runs it is passionate about the business and this is dependent on the passion the business owner is in the products or services they are providing. There is no way that you can succeed in a company which you do not have a love for, and that's why it is important to pick the kind of business you invest in with care. You must be proud of the product you're selling because it will determine how to be

able to present the product to your clients and convince them to buy it. Network marketing isn't something that you just do for a couple of months after that you get rid of it. Imagine working for a long time , but you don't enjoy it in the least? It is important to ensure that you're enthusiastic about the products you sell in order to remain in the business for a longer period and working hard to get customers into your network and making more sales each day.

Provide testimonials-

Trust is an essential factor in every business. Customers will prefer doing business with a name or a person they believe in. Through testimonials, potential customers will be able to see what type of businessperson you are, which will help them trust you more. Testimonials can help you reach out to those who are seeking businesspeople like you. Through testimonials, many people will be interested in what you're dealing with. Tell about your experiences and successes too, and a lot of people will feel connected to you.

The use of TV ads

A lot of people watch television across the nation and there are times that people have more television than other times.Advertisers put their ads in those times, knowing that lots of people are watching TV. This is the time when you put your ad also, so that you can draw the attention of potential network marketers who might be interested in the subject you're dealing with. Take advantage of advertising traffic and place your advertisement where you're certain that a lot of people will be able to view it.Good news is that nowadays there are a lot of people looking into network marketing while looking for an affordable method to begin a company that could generate an income that can supplement the one you already earn. This is the reason they could consider your advert.

Chapter 11: Keep Focus On Competitive Landscape

It is beneficial to have a little competition for any company, particularly when it is related to networking marketing. If a company of similar size is established the next building, there's enough space that both companies can be in existence at present. The company you compete with is likely the greatest factor in your growth. Why? You can gain knowledge from the strategies they employ by studying their strengths, weaknesses, and strategies. If you look at some of the world's most successful individuals including entrepreneurs, athletes and CEO's. You will see that they have taken the time to research their competitors and know the factors that make them tick. But, in order to make the most of the strategies of your competitors it is essential to understand exactly what to search for. Because you're not trying to take their ideas or copy their product, you need their strategies and the reasons behind employing certain strategies for selling.

Copycats are not the way to beat your rivals. If you simply copy what your competitor does, you'll always be ahead. But if you examine their actions and comprehend why they make the choices they make, you'll be able to identify lucrative opportunities that you might have missed. Begin by looking up the opinions of others about your competition to help further the development of your product and enhance your service. What can their mistakes and successes assist you in developing your sales strategies and enhance them? If you hear complaints from customers about the quality and usability or cost of products from your competition You will be able to identify the areas that your business could improve on. It's that simple. Your customers are aware of what they want and if you observe and modify your business, they will turn to you to meet their needs.

The failures of your competitors should not be the sole motivation to alter your sales strategies. Success of a competitor is equally important as you can discover the things your company is not doing right. If you can see what your competition is doing well and listen to customers raving of their experiences, you're getting direct information about what your customer is searching for. This means that you'll be able to meet this. Insofar as your strategy is superior and more effective, you'll be able to become the most reliable source for your client's requirements.

Making a steady income

You've joined a business that is a network marketing and have begun to make sales. You are seeing rapid growth and you've finally started to pay back the amount you invested in the beginning. Nowis the time to step up your game and take life-changing steps. Many people join network marketing as a means to earn extra money while working a 9-5 job. However, the most successful network marketers are able to effectively create their own business as the sole revenue source. Network marketing will give you the opportunity to pursue your goals through allowing you to be in control by allowing you to work from home and financial freedom. Why do you have to spend the rest of your life working on someone who is not yours when you can work at your own pace and enjoy earn an unlimited amount of money. You choose the length of time you'd like to be at it and the amount of effort you invest into selling.

Your success is merited in their own right but your failures will be attributed to your perseverance and dedication. With enough motivation and determination you can make an income that is steady and sustainable through network marketing.

How do you start your transition from a regular occupation to one that is network-based? The good news is that this chapter provides steps that assist you on your way to financial freedom. But, you can't take the spur of the moment and make a leap of faith into the realm that is network marketing. It is necessary to establish an income that is stable for at minimum six months before you can say goodbye to work.

Step 1: Select an appropriate product line to market your network marketing business. For example: nutrition. Network marketing companies that focus on nutrition growing in popularity by the second. However, as diets that are trendy as well as obesity and fast food chains grow and spread, people will always be in need of an option for health-related products and services.

Step 2: Once you've discovered your idea for a product, you need to search for a wholesaler to purchase from. The National Association of Wholesaler-Distributors offer many high quality companies to make your purchases from. Go to Naw.org to take a take a look at their list of trustworthy names. You can also join free trade publications by visiting Tradepub.com for additional sources.

Step 3: Connect with potential wholesalers and distributors of manufacturers. Ask them about drop-shipping options and if they have suppliers catalogs and order forms for the items. Of course, you should pick the distributor who offers you the lowest price per item.

Step 4: Once you've finally discovered a vendor and have a supplier, you need to create your own sales plan. You must decide on the price at which you will sell your products, however, keep in mind that the price you set should be in line with the suggestions of your supplier's sales. Choose a commission plan for your distributors at different levels. For instance, you could set commission of ten percent for the first-level reps that is, the distributor earns cash from the products the team sells.

Step 5: Write an instruction guideline for your sales representatives and distributors, with a variety of methods to promote your brand new company's network marketing. Create an inventory kit to allow your employees to market products that they like and are easy to use. The kit should include examples, instructions for a catalog, pricing and orders forms.

Step 6: Begin to advertise once you've identified employees and have products for sale. You can reach out to newspapers, magazines and radio stations, farmers' markets, and even local businesses to help your growing company. Make use of all the methods which were described in chapter three.

Step 7 7. Now is the best moment to contact your customers directly regardless of whether you bought an item online and in person. If someone is interested in your advertisement, then send an individual brochure, sales letter and an order form. If a potential client calls your business number to inquire more details regarding your offerings, offer them a phone call.

Understanding Taxes

Now, you've successfully started your successful career in network marketing and earned a substantial amount of money. However, like any other venture there's a looming aspect that you're left with to deal with tax obligations. Everyone is terrified of the word "tax but as a first-time self-employed marketer and business owner you need to carefully research and be aware of each aspect in preparing and recording taxes that you pay for your network marketing company. There are three kinds of federal taxes that affect network marketers such as income tax, self-employment tax and employment tax. The majority of your tax details will be reported on a tax form 1040 as well as its subsequent parts such as Schedule A for deductions that are itemized and Schedule C for loss or profit and Schedule C- Eaz for net profits along with schedule SE in self-employment tax.

Taxes on employment are exclusively applicable for network marketing companies who employ employees to be employed by them. For specific requirements to determine whether someone working for you is considered to be an employee to authorities of the United States government, consult the IRS Revenue ruling 87-41. You can also contact 800-TAX-FORM for further information.

Because of the increasing individuals leaving the job to go home or to become self-employed due to the rise in self-employment, the IRS was forced to review the types of breaks and deductions to offer these entrepreneurs. In 1999 the IRS permitted home-based businesses to be considered deductions, in order to increase the appeal of tax planning to those who run a network marketing. So, if your business of network marketing is your primary source of income, you may be eligible for number of tax benefits that are available to all business owners.

Tax deductions are something you should be thrilled about and eagerly anticipate but there's some negative information regarding the network marketing industry and taxes. There are numerous tax codes or regulations and interpretations that can seriously affect the small-scale business you run. Each of these regulations play an crucial roles in your tax return as an owner of a business. It is therefore essential to know and comprehend each aspect of your tax filing so that you don't get in difficulties in the eyes of IRS. The IRS declares that you are not able to take deductions for certain business expenses in the event that you are using the circumstances to make a profit not just for an interest. How do you determine what the IRS will judge your business? The IRS will apply two criteria to determine its position that is the first one: whether you've made an income within three of the five years. The other is if you can prove to them that you have purposely used your business to earn an income that is significant. In this scenario the IRS is looking into whether you conduct your company in a professional way and invest the required effort and time to help the business succeed, and how much you depend on the revenue generated by your business to sustain your lifestyle.

Food as well as Entertainment Network marketing requires you to interact personally with your customers. Sometimes, this means winning and eating with them. However, while you take clients out for a meal but you'll also have to eat to sustain yourself. You'll be on traveling a lot trying to find new members as well as sell your products. Entertainment and dining is one cost that

IRS is able to cut down. The deductions you can claim are restricted to a maximum of fifty percent of your meals and entertainment expenses. In this situation it is important to keep track of your entertainment and meal costs as deductable expenses. Not only do you need to include your receipts but also the documentation of the discussion in the business that took place at the time, as well as relationships with business partners (who you dined with).

Home Office Deduction

You are fortunate enough to count your home office space as an exemption from taxes. However, you should be prepared to prove the way you utilize the space you have for your office. If your office is in compliance with the requirements you are able to take a deduction of a certain percentage of expenses that are connected to the entire home. This could include home's mortgage and utility bills, as well as repairs, and home insurance. The office space needs to be used frequently and solely to run your company. There is no other central location for your managerial or administrative tasks.

Regular Business Costs

The expenses listed above are what you'd expect the business costs are. You can deduct expenses like: accounting fees, license fees, advertising fees, etc. The biggest benefit when it comes to taxes in this situation is that your private life and your professional life may overlap. You are able to deduct phone bills, office supplies computers, fax machines, cleaning products and services as well as office furniture and even decorations. It's a fantastic chance to benefit from the tax deductions that are available and to improve your work-life balance.

Networking and Travel

As a network marketing professional, you must travel in order to connect with distributors, customers and potential recruits. However, if you have an interest in travel or your spouse enjoys travel, then you could make use of your worldly experience to market your business in network marketing. Business travel deductions are one of the most significant benefits of network marketing. However, you need to be able to prove your business travel being related regardless of your travel ventures. There's a hazy line in the legality of your travel as a part of your business of network marketing. For instance within the United States, all of your travel expenses are tax-deductible if your travel is solely to conduct business. However, when you travel abroad it is important to divide the expenses of travel between business and leisure.

Of course, as spring rolls around, so does tax season. You must spend some time during your busy schedule to complete forms and determine what the IRS must know. Nearly every wholesale network marketing distributor agreement recognizes your status being an individual contractor and the IRS. Because of the IRS accepting your status as a self-employed businessperson that you must pay self-employment tax and income tax as well as tax. If you earn over five hundred dollars in a year, then you need to be paying tax quarterly. If you earn over six hundred bucks per year or buy more than five thousand dollars worth of products, then you'll be required to submit an Form 1099. The form is attached with you Schedule C, along with your tax return. The Schedule C will summarize your expenses and income from the company that offers network marketing.

Assets: Cars, computers and Capital

In regards to your assets, you'll definitely need to consult your tax professional for a personalized consultation. It is necessary to make some important decisions regarding what you can claim as a deduction for the costs for purchasing your computer, equipment as well as vehicles that are used solely to run your business network. The IRS is fairly flexible and expansive limitations on the amount you are able to claim as a business deduction an individual year. However, the cost of your assets are only limited to the earnings that you earn through your business. There is also the option of taking the benefit of depreciation over several years for certain items of business equipment. This information should be decided by your tax adviser.

The expenses of your vehicle specifically designed for your company's network marketing are actually tax-deductible. But, you are able to take these deductions into one of two methods. The IRS's guidelines of cents-per-mile or you can itemize the expenses of your car: gas maintenance, depreciation and maintenance repairs and insurance can be all deducted, if appropriate. However, it is important to have to determine the proportion of your total vehicle usage in relation to your company's network marketing and adjust the record of these costs accordingly.

The most important thing to remember is that with regards to your business in the field of network marketing and tax obligations, you should keep detailed records about your costs. If you are able to meet with the lovely employees of the IRS They will inform you that keeping accurate documentation of deductions can aid in proving your claims. Since company expenses represent the sole deductions that you are able to claim on your tax returns You should think about creating a separate bank account specifically for the expenses. It is also important to keep track of each business transaction and save the documents. Receipts, in this instance, are the most convincing evidence for proving the business's expenditures.

Conclusion

The industry of network marketing has witnessed an increase in the number of employees because people are becoming aware of the advantages network marketing can offer against traditional model of businesses. A lot of companies across the globe employ network marketing to their advantage due to its efficiency as a model for business.

In the course of your life, you'll have met at least one person who is familiar in network marketing. If you're reading this book, you are fascinated by the concept of network marketing, as it's a method to achieve financial freedom or perhaps because you've been a part of the growing ranks professional network marketers. Keep in mind that your journey to success doesn't end when you become a distributor. Understanding the insides and outs of the characteristics that make network marketing distinctive knowing the best strategies to be successful as a network marketing professional and approaching your endeavor with a positive mindset can go a long way toward surviving in the fast-paced, ever-changing world.

Equally important to knowing the basics in network marketing is investing your entire effort to becoming successful in this industry will help you achieve success. Your attitude, character and conduct will determine whether you succeed or failure. The most fundamental element for network marketing lies in establishing connections with others so that you can provide them with information and education about what you can provide. This requires the necessary interpersonal skills as you encounter a variety of individuals regular basis.

To create an online network and establish relationships that can help you on the path of achieving your goals, you need a specific sort of person, one who is able to see the big picture and has the right mindset. You're definitely one of them otherwise, you would not have bought this book and read to this point.

Based on everything you've learned in this book you'll have the confidence to step out and start building your network. Only after taking the first step towards success will you be able to realize your goals. Congratulations for taking the first step!

Thank you for taking the time to read this book. I wish you a lot of success on your way. Be focused and continue to move ahead!